# THE KNOPF POETRY SERIES

# CATS OF THE
# TEMPLE

# CATS OF THE TEMPLE

POEMS BY

BRAD LEITHAUSER

ALFRED A. KNOPF  NEW YORK  1986

Acknowledgments: "The Buried Graves," "Recollections of an Irish Daybreak," "In a Bonsai Nursery," "A Stuffed Tortoise," "In Minako Wada's House," "A Flight from Osaka" and "Seaside Greetings" originally appeared in *The New Yorker;* "Two Suspensions Against a Blacktop Backdrop" (originally entitled "Two Suspensions"), "Rabbits," "The Tigers of Nanzen-ji" and "In a Japanese Moss Garden" in *The Atlantic Monthly;* "A Noisy Sleeper," "Two Incidents on and off Guam," "Floating Light in Tokyo" and "At Greg's" in *The New Criterion;* "An Actor Plays a Trumpet" and "Seahorses" in *The New York Review of Books;* "Hesitancy" in *The New Republic;* "On a Seaside Mountain" in *Harper's.* "Post-Coitum Tristesse: A Sonnet" (originally entitled "Post-Coital Depression: A Sonnet") appeared, along with a short statement on poetic form, in *Epoch.* The poems in the third section of this book, with the exception of "At Greg's," appeared in 1985 as a chapbook, *A Seaside Mountain,* published by The Sarabande Press.

LIBRARY OF CONGRESS CATALOGING IN PUBLICATION DATA

Leithauser, Brad.
Cats of the temple.
(Knopf poetry series ; 20)
I. Title.
PS3562.E4623C3   1986   811'.54   85-40228
ISBN 0-394-54806-x
ISBN 0-394-74152-8 (pbk.)

To John Chapman,
*another brother*

Obliging readers will greet this book as a sibling companion to my first, *Hundreds of Fireflies*. Although I am eager to dedicate my work to teachers and friends, a distaste for any intervening words between a poem's title and text—even an epigraph—compels me to tuck away my gratitude here. With retiring but plentiful thanks, then, "Two Suspensions Against a Blacktop Backdrop" is dedicated to Carolyn Cyran, "The Buried Graves" to David Sofield, "An Actor Plays a Trumpet" to William Pritchard, "Rabbits" to Richard Lyon, "In a Bonsai Nursery" to Joseph and Janet Phillips, "Two Incidents on and off Guam" to Albert and Janet Salter, "Floating Light in Tokyo" to James Merrill, "Hesitancy" to Anthony Hecht, "At Greg's" to Scott Mead, "In Minako Wada's House" to Dr. and Mrs. Kikugo Masuda, "The Tigers of Nanzen-ji" to Dr. Zentaro Kitagawa, "In a Japanese Moss Garden" to Ann Close, "A Flight from Osaka" to Katsuyuki Kumano and "Seaside Greetings" to Mary Jo Salter.

I have been the happy recipient of a number of financial awards, and must lastly thank the John Simon Guggenheim Foundation, Mr. Brinton P. Roberts and the other Trustees of the Amy Lowell Poetry Travelling Scholarship, the Ingram Merrill Foundation and the John D. and Catherine T. MacArthur Foundation for their inspiriting and liberating support.

# CONTENTS

# CATS OF THE
# TEMPLE

# TWO SUSPENSIONS
# AGAINST A BLACKTOP BACKDROP

Straight up noon, I watch a toad
  —dusty, huge—cross a blacktop road
by hops and halts; landing each
    time like a splattered
egg, he regathers, heavily pauses
  in the baking sun, and heaves
aloft again, again until he makes
  the road's shoulder, come
    to rest finally under some
dusty asparagus leaves.


Next—and from nowhere,
    from right out of the air—
  quick as thought
    drops a damselfly,
the wings that keep
  her motionless an icy blur
of motion. . . . Each at each appeared
  to peer: he maybe held
    by the sun-enameled
emerald stickpin of her

spare torso; she,
   by a stolidity
so extreme it looks
   accomplished, a dumb but deep-
rooted contentment. Perhaps,
   of course, this choice encounter
wasn't one and their gazes
   never met; yet they seemed to,
      at least for a few
suspensive seconds that were—


   were, obscurely, reminiscent of
      a web I'd found just above
   my head that same summer, which,
      metaphor for memory
turned selfless, by a trick
   of the light had altogether
vanished, yielding to the eye
   but what incidence had blown there:
      some seeds, needles, threadbare
leaves, a curled gray feather—

were, surely, irresistible grist
　　for the fabulist,
who might well conclude
　　that each, true to the instant's
instance, as it urged the
　　resolution of mind and mass,
had felt the other's opposed
　　appeals, and however much
　　*could* pass between two such
contrary creatures indeed did pass.

# THE BURIED GRAVES

From the pier, at dusk, the dim
    Billowing arms of kelp
Seem the tops of trees, as though
    Not long ago
A summer wood stood here, before a dam
    Was built, a valley flooded.


Such a forest would release
    Its color only slowly,
And the leafy branches sway, as they'd
    More lightly swayed
Under a less distant sun and far less
    Even weather. Now, deeper down,


Those glimmers of coral might
    Be the lots of some hard-luck
Town, or—depositing on the dead
    A second bed—
A submerged cemetery. . . . To this mute,
    Envisioned, birdless wood would


Come a kind of autumn, a tame
    Sea-season, with foliage tumbling
Through a weighty, trancelike fall;
    And come, as well,
Soon in the emptying fullness of time,
    A mild but an endless winter.

# AN ACTOR PLAYS A TRUMPET

What comes through
in this rooftop conclusion to an old movie
in which somebody who
clearly doesn't know how to play it
picks up a banged-up trumpet
to play against a light-hung screen
meant to represent
a metropolitan skyline

is some sense
of the soaring and transformative strength
of jazz. When he plants
his bandaged shoes, cocks his boyish profile
and lifts the horn to ride a gorgeous roll
of dubbed spontaneity, the effect is (despite
that bogus clothesline at
his back, with its one limp sheet)

persuasive:
those high, ramping notes speak of daring,
the flutter-throated vibrato of
diffidence, and the whole of unformed
invention, wound yet in the horn's warmed-
up cerebric densities. Indeed, so fine
is the music, even his
acting's better for it and as the camera tracks in

on the sure
kiss at the tiny mouthpiece, you might
almost believe that here
is a man whose upper lip burns, night
after night, in the effort
to make unpremeditation look
easy. Although he's
turning his back on the city, the music

is a gift
to its boxed-in inhabitants: the loose,
looping melodies waft
over the roof's edge, falling,
and, in falling, joining
that collected world of objects you've watched
falling on film—all
the briefcases and rifles and bottles pitched

from tower
and cliff-top, the beribboned packets
of love-letters lofted over
the rails of ocean liners, the open buckets
of paint, the key rings and miner's flashlights,
the flying anvils and leather-upholstered
convertibles and sun
hats and muddied sacks of gold. . . . Gold

as the moon
ought to be, the pounded streets, the lumpen
    heart that weights a man,
stooping his shoulders—just that fleeting,
flyaway color are the tones tonight lighting
    off his horn. And when a slow
        coldness blows in, a gold-
    to-blue harmonic shift, oh


        he's dying
up there with the fit sweetness of it,
        digging hard, as with a shovel, going
deep for the ultimate, most intimate
strain in his chest. The multi-storied, tight-
    plotted metropolis at his feet,
        coruscating all the more
    for the yearnings he lays upon it,


        would topple
if he hurled his trumpet at it.

# DAINTIES: A SUITE

## *I. Recollections of an Irish Daybreak*

Dawn in its high-
flung overtones
alights upon
the hilltops first,
descending by
warming degrees
slopes still nearer
silver than green
as the sun lifts
and the sea takes
on then loses
its scumbling blue,
lavender, rose
and peach glazes;

sprung aerial
arousals, big
bulging reaches'
enkindlings come
seasonably
down to grounded
unveilings that
lighten but lend
no color to
all of the gray
stone walls that spill
with the smoothed trends
of streams down each
responsive hill.

And while, up close,
these walls are seen
as nothing more
than reject moons,
or misshapen
skulls of a lax,
superseded
race that left in
terms of remains
nothing but its
bones, they display
to someone at
a sufficient
distance—to, say,

a young man perched
commandingly
on a boulder
whose barnacle-
gripped, weed-strung base
the sea rinses—
all of the live,
slung fluency
of spider's thread.
How handsomely
from his select
vantage (with a
zigzag jigsaw
puzzle effect)

the whole terrain
has come to be
overlain by
one extended
web, in whose most
ample, fertile
interstices
fields are tended,
cattle fatten,
chimneys project
their indolent
and indirect
assault upon
the firmament.

## II. Rabbits: A Valentine

Deliberate
on the rabbit,
who if what you
hear is half true
has found the way
to inhabit
a world without
elaborate
courtship, yet one
flushed with piquant
concupiscent
satisfaction,
a world whose slack
meadowed moments
sit suspended
between frequent
bouts of rabid
raptured action . . .
males of splendid
near-heroic
virility,
females of a
commensurate,
magnificent
fertility.

Ponder this shy
but quite able
go-get-'er, for
whom even sex
is not complex,
who meets and mates,
and keeps no count
but sees the flesh-
of-his-flesh both
diversify
and multiply;
who does not tire
for long, and with
the great outdoors
as his table
banquets on fresh
greens as he waits
for the desire
to mount to mount.

Consider this
suitor of sorts
who advocates
a direct style,
who's sharp on fun-
damentals and
in a twinkling,
his little heart
kicking, is hard
at it; who gets
and forgets while
composing no
explanations,
damnations, grand
pleadings or vows—
disengages
and instantly
begins to browse,
lifting to all
eyes his eyes (oh,
those lovable
black bunny eyes!)
innocent and
intelligent.

Nearly nothing
in Nature so
spirits the eye
off—but off by
way of in—to
unveil detail
as minimal
as it's recep-
tive to as does
this more than true-

to-life, living
family of
diminutive
replicas of
themselves, whose pin-
point blossomings
and punctual
leaf-losses, whose
every nubbled
knob and fissure,

knot-imploded
distension and
deep, thematic
torsion reproach
our recognized
but unrenounced
confusion of
size with grandeur.

These pondered, hand-
won triumphs of
containment, come,
tentatively,
of earth-toughened
fingers, father
to son, and on
to son, so long
as the branches
hold on each side,

bid us enter-
tain notions of
days whose hours are
shorter than ours
(shrunken, misted,
mossed-in seasons,
amassed in hard-
pressed heartwood rings) . . .
and enter, please,
a forest where

sun, planets, stars,
and our little
still-swollen moon
are brought, though yet
unreachable,
nearer the roofs
of the trim, smoke-
puffing houses.

# ON THE LEE SIDE

Two hours along,
the wind the whole time rising,
I find the site—and seat—for which
it seems I have been looking:

a hip-sized hollow
on the lee side of a low
but broad-boled pine, above a blue-gray,
fretted inlet, with a distant view

of a blue-black,
icily whitecapped sea. I settle my pack
on the ground beside me. It holds, within,
an apple, a green plum, a handbook

in which I might
pin down precisely what
sort of pine now harbors me, a map
that likewise would set me straight

as to how far,
so far, I've pursued my longings for
the peninsula's roundabout Point,
and some expensive new rain-gear

which, unless that
thunderheaded cloudbank's set
farther off, offshore, I'll need before long.
But not yet. So I leave it shut,

and shut my eyes.
Dimly, after a bit, I seem to recognize
the sweep of broken water on rock,
but for the most part the sea's

   struggles are drowned
beneath big, shattering waves of sound
as the wind floods in among the trees,
making the knotted branches bend

   so painfully
backward, the hurt released in high
disjointed creakings. Hands pocketed, eyes
closed wide on darkness, it's as though

   my hearing now
sharpens by degrees, until I can follow,
it would nearly seem, down every threaded
aerial pathway overhead, the flow

   of each succeeding
gust—rising, and at length retreating
through shifting tons of needles,
and always while retreating bundling

   steadily closer
those storm-cloud masses. And what a pleasure,
to hear the wind pitch still higher, to know
the waves swell and fall in answer,

blindly to feel
the whole sky blackening! Given my all-
but-absolute sense of shelter here,
perched on the rim of colossal

    upheaval in
perfect safety, I can scarcely come down
hard on that elusive but unavoidable, queer
but predictable inner companion

    who asks for nothing
save that his each fresh-formulated craving
meet some delivered satisfaction
that needs no waiting,

    who breeds an air
of collected mystery through sheer
indifference to others' welfare, and who's
neatly, snugly sure

    just how this splendid
show of weather's to be accounted for:
ingenious exhibitions exclusively intended
to entice and entertain him here.

# A STUFFED TORTOISE

Inwardly re-outfitted over a century ago
according to the handwritten, yellow
three-by-five directly below
the lunging neck, he is, among this petrified
    menagerie, just as once in life,

the oldest of animals. The armadillo
beside him, the Manx cat, the dartlike row
of birds along the wall, all look as though
they never were alive, but whoever re-posed
    our tortoise attended to that

tension which makes him — with the frog and fox — so
didactically adaptable: Who can resist the slow-
paced, cumulative humor of this low-
profiled plodder, who somehow sweeps
    the big races, speaks volumes by example only,

and, fetchingly shy, zeroes inward at any show
of attention — and yet whose narrow,
near-panicky glance is that of some desperado
on the lam? The neck strains, *forward,*
    as if that tough, undersized head

yearned to outstrip its ponderous cargo.
— The time's not ripe for that? If so, the true
burden on his back may be years which offer no
movement casual or quick enough to escape
    a painstaking, on-the-spot review.

# MINIMS

### Manifest Destiny

Now if, somehow, offered a brand-new New
World, an endless, arable *tabula rasa*,
Wouldn't we dedicate that one, too, to
The billboard, the smokestack, the shopping plaza?


### That Trojan Horse

It pretty much stinks,
though it may be only human—
the way Man looks at Woman
and secretly thinks,
You've got to believe
it's better to give than to receive.


### At a Formal Do

Rouge-cheeked Rhyme, that hoary matchmaker,
    Clasps a young man's hand—and squeezes.
"I've someone for you to meet who will
    Take your breath away," she wheezes.
"An angel—true! A vision of delight!"

    *Jay* to *May, Will* to *Jill,*
    She pairs them off all night.

*The Fame Train*

The season's major talents are
  Roaring up the track.
You can hear them coming: clique
  Claque, clique claque.


*Post-Coitum Tristesse: A Sonnet*

Why
do
you
sigh,
roar,
fall,
all
for
some
hum-
drum
come
—mm?
Hm . . .

*"Well Then How About Saturday?"*

Rather than assistance,
This one seeks resistance—
   Given her kiss and blessing,
   Finds the impulse detumescing.


*The Haunted*

A crying white candle
   Lights the room where
The moon's fairest woman
   Brushes her hair
And we who are dying
   Just to be near her,
Who inextricably
   Adore and fear her,

Hurl ourselves flatly
   On the walls and floor,
Dancing a love-dance
   More and more
Frenzied until—a kind
   Of kiss—she places
Her mouth to the flame, and
   Blows out our faces.

*Freudian Slip*

With this turnabout
a wild brain-child
is beguiled
out;

when at last the wits
relent, the self
reveals its-
elf.


*Poet's Lament*

Why must gainful
Employment be so painful?

# SEAHORSES

Kin to all kinds
Of fancied hybrids—minotaur
And wyvern, cockatrice,
Kyrin and griffin—this
Monkey-tailed, dragon-chested
Prankish twist of whimsy
Outshines that whole composited
Menagerie, for this sequined
Equine wonder, howsoever
Improbably,

Quite palpably
Exists! Within his moted
Medium, tail loosely laced
Round the living hitching post
Of a coral twig, he feeds at leisure
As befits a mild, compromising
Creature with no arms of defense
Save that of, in his knobby
Sparsity, appearing
Unappetizing.

Like that chess piece
He so resembles, he glides
  With a forking, oblique
Efficiency, the winglike
Fins behind his ears aflutter;
  And like that lone
Unmastered steed to whom
The word-weary everywhere
  Look for replenishment—
  That is to say, our own


  Like-winged, light-winged
Pegasus—he can be taken
  As an embodiment
Of the obscure fount
And unaccountable buoyancy
  Of artistic inspiration.
Yet defined by neither,
Finally, by nothing afloat
  On the long, circulating
  Seas of creation,

Is this mailed male
Who bears in his own brood pouch
   A female's transferred conceptions,
And seems to move (those fins
By turns transparent) through
   Telekinetic promptings, while his
Turreted, nonsynchronous
Eyes are taking in two
   Views at once. How appropriate
      That gaze of his is—


      For he conveys
A sense of living at least two
   Simultaneous lives, of always
Having a mucilaginous
If metaphorical foot
   Planted in a neighboring, renum-
bered dimension, one whose
Dim-sensed presence releases our
   Ineffable but hopeful
      Yearnings for some

Further release.
In his otherworldliness
    He heartens us. . . . If there's to be
Any egress for you and me
From the straitening domain
    Of the plausible, what course
More likely than astride the plated
Shoulders of this shimmering
    Upright swimmer, this
        Waterbound winged horse?

# A NOISY SLEEPER

*I. 1958*

The noisy sleeper
in the other room is my
Grandfather whose snores go up & down
up & down like a zipper. Deeper


deeper for the dark
his big breathing climbs
& slips away
like the moon like the day


like Cinny who I so
much wanted to stay
here with me in a bed too big
for me. But Cinny when I let her go


was gone
on her clicking toes
in blackness with the thin slits
open on her black nose


and not a shiver in her chest
for what out there just might
be waiting. She lies at ease I know
on a floor in the night

body curled completely
in the safety of a ring
in whose fur center her head
fits neatly.

In his desk for luck he keeps
an Indian head
penny with the date
he was born which is 1898.

He promised he will look
for one for luck for me
which is 1953.
Whatever

could be that's wrong
what is needed I know
is to be watchful to be strong
simply

though such breathing's far
too big for this house in which
he & I together are
sleeping and I do not sleep.

Recalling now
From the subsiding brink
Of earliest memory
The night-sounds of that man,
My grandfather, is to see
How even at age five one can
Accept reassurances as though
They were believable while
Darkly continuing to think
Things over—to see how
Soon the mind learns to reconcile
Itself to a complex ignorance,
As one begins to know

One does not know.
Now whatever that unnamed
Crisis actually was which placed me
In that giant's bed that night
(Illness in the family?
Some remote, unheard-of fight?
Or, likelier, a disaster lifted
From the blaze of a small boy's inflamed
Imagination . . . ) it passed
Much as night passes into dawn,
Unobserved and at last,
Leaving no trace as it drifted
Wholly out of mind. Gone—

Like the existence
Of all others in that house. No doubt
My grandmother was there, too,
Sleeping or, like me, pretending
To sleep, but I don't recall
Her presence, or anyone who
Played with me that day, or what fell out
The next. No, in memory
It's simply two people all
Alone, my grandfather and me,
Bound across the distance
Of a night that rises
And falls and has no ending.

But given all
Memory's shortcomings, one still must
Marvel at its power to restore
The feel of that small boy's fears,
Or the way it can take an old man
Dead now some twenty years
And hold him up close enough
To overhear the rise and fall
Of his slow breathing, just
As though his were once more
The sort of sleep from which—broken
By ruminative snorts, gruff
Assentive gasps—he could be woken.

# TWO INCIDENTS ON AND OFF GUAM

*I.*

Nothing was going to seem very
Strange after that extraordinary
Drive down to the beach in the back
Of a jeep, the road snaking
Through huge cross-sections of jungle even
Denser than what we'd seen before,
Uppermost fronds a dazzling, rich
White-bronze in that tropical sun, gray
Those farther down, and nearly black
The warring undergrowth in which
Windfall coconuts lay
Like so many old, flaking
Helmets from that other War;

So that, when we found everyone
On the beach standing right
At the water's edge, watching the sea,
We fell in unquestioningly,
Gazes drifting until we too
Spotted in the distance, where
The sea was whitecapped, a pair
Of bobbing swimmers. They
Were drowning. A simple truth—but one
We couldn't grasp at first, nor quite
Grasp that the only thing to do
Was to stand and wait. A radio
Call had gone out. . . . Help was on the way.

Help, at last, took the splendid,
Hearteningly larger-than-life form
Of a helicopter ripping across
The sky to come to a high, suspended
Clattering halt and release a fine
Rope ladder that landed just outside
The swimmers' reach. Now commenced
That clumsy, exacting process—so
Brutally, so agonizingly slow—
Of attempts at linkage; each new toss
Of the ladder falling wide,
As the fading swimmers flailed against
The pull of their local storm,

Until somehow, as we stood there
Watching, that deep, tortuous bond between
Man the maker and his machine
Was pared to a dangling thread,
And right before our eyes a half-dead
Body like a fish was hoisted through
The glittering, naked air
To the copter's belly—leaving two
All but disembodied arms to thrash
In the sunny scatter and smash,
The stunned smash and scatter of the sea.
    Now horrifying, hypnotizing
As this was, it was, finally,

Unreal as well, as though
We were watching a film-clip, some
Snippet of the evening news . . .
The entire ordeal—the bare
Line dropped again, then again, and then
That second swimmer delivered from
His gasping burial—at once so
Stirring, and so *unreal:*
Even as we yelled, whistled, clapped
Our hands, somehow still to feel,
As in a moviehouse, that we'd been
Played on by a drama whose
Performers were never there.


*II.*


The rubber feet pinch,
the window of the mask is scratched. Easing
out of my element, I inch
down the aluminum ladder

on the side of the boat,
legs trailing loose in the warm sea,
let go, drop and turn and float
successfully on my stomach. I send a blast

of air up the snorkel, spouting a crown
of salty water that, after
a looping pause, comes down
sweetly on my back, and begin, flush

with the reserved, lazing
powers of my new frog's feet, to coast
upon the surface. Under this blazing
noon sun the sea's so calm it can scarcely be

the medium in which, just three days ago,
those two swimmers I keep thinking about
were nearly drowned. The water's so
tranquil today you could swim out

for miles, it seems, letting it hold
you high like a child, aloft and kicking
in a parent's upraised arms. Assorted spilled
pastels, dissolved of all

material commitments, flicker and glide
in the bay's upper reaches;
today the sea's wide-
open and the sun goes clear

to the rolling coral stone-
garden, some forty feet below, where
three divers in black wet-suits, two men
and the boyishly slighter

figure of a woman, drift to and fro,
poking about, exchanging
sweeping, emphatic messages by way
of hand-signals. As enticing

as that sea-floor looks, still
more so—a grace to place
against any anemone's—are those tall
wavering columns of bubbles

rising from the divers' air-tanks;
while risibly like the thought-balloons
one meets in comic books
and animated cartoons, they possess

a lissomeness, a vinelike
elevating loveliness that pulls me
closer. And when I flutter-kick
over to where the bubbles break

the surface, nosing my mask right
into that climbing line of hundreds
and hundreds of spirited white
beads of light

something marvelous transpires: I am—again—
reminded of film, the colorless
televisions of my boyhood, that endless run
of laugh-tracked comedies in which

with some low-budget hocus-pocus
(the camera, to the strum of a harp,
slipping out of focus,
or a panning swing toward the center

of a painted target- or pin-
wheel-shape that would then
begin to spin)
one was forever being promoted

to those selective sectors
where cumulus banks are firm enough
for walking, a white sheet is every actor's
home- and office-apparel alike, and one finds

each humble face laughably
unaltered—bespectacled or buck-toothed,
bald or bulbous-nosed as the case may be, but *happy*,
for this is Heaven. . . . And to this vision

while I floated simply
in the upsurge of a stranger's
exhalations, body limply
open to the sea's slight suggestive nudgings,

came another, of which the first, for all
its silliness, was a kind of clue, a parody
whose unsullied original
might be obliquely

glanced at, indeed
had been glimpsed already,
for there was a sense of having peered
before into one of these

miraculous pristine

passages that wait beside you
always, if only it were known *which*
floorboard to take the crowbar to,
*which* stone uproot on the hillside, if only

you dared to; *this* tunnel, here, into a breath-
taking incandescence so intense the
body is as nothing in the path
of its streaming, weightless and homeless and

helpless, hopeful and afraid.

# FLOATING LIGHT IN TOKYO

Having lost track of the time in your own
country, how long you've been up, how little
you slept on the plane, but finding yourself alone
in a small room in an enormous city

you take the elevator down to the dim
lobby and feeling just like a criminal slip
out for a walk beside the moated rim
of the Imperial Palace. It's late—

even the packed, desperate thoroughfares
of Central Tokyo are all but deserted.
Vistas have opened up, and the air's
cooled a bit at last. You can hear

a few horns honking in the distance,
also a heavy truck which, meeting
strong internal resistance,
manfully strains and strains as it climbs

into gear and rumbles off. Such sounds
deepen rather than deplete the sensation
of an enchanted spell of sleep that extends
over miles and millions. Yet it's you

who's about to awaken, as a bend in the moat
reveals a vision—enchanted, too—
of frenzy: a jeweled inner city afloat
in light, the mad neon dazzle of the Ginza. . . .

43

The neon blazes cleanly in the old moat.
Lights on lights are overlaid in repeated
applications which soothe somewhat
a staggered, jet-lagged brain that longs

to rest yet somehow can't; for they fill
the mind as dreams do, these flourishing
ribbons on the ebony flux, the spill
of moons, keys and horns, the many-petaled rose

and amber and azure blooms that flare
and fade, flare and fade in rocking
even rhythms. How pleasing they are!—
these emblems from a Halloween magician's cape,

these colors selected for brightness alone,
recalling jars of fingerpaint on the low shelves
of a primary classroom. With regret, then,
you note an approaching duck, whose wake shivers

all reflections; and it hurts a little
to watch the neat incision being cut, the plush
collapse begin as the first nudging ripple
swings outwards. Yet as the duck, in passing,

transforms into a swan, the shapely *S*
of the neck lit in sudden fluorescent profile,
and familiar designs begin to coalesce
within the moat, which soon again will reflect

composedly, you'll grant that while the static
glaze was restful, welcome is this
queen of birds with the sea-serpentine neck,
who trails behind her such thrilling rubble.

# HESITANCY

For a start here's hesitancy
played on a breezy afternoon
    at the Kyoto Zoo by an
ostrich met with the offer
    of a pretzel: a pink two-toed
stalking to the fence, there to pin
    upon the quailing child
        the enlarged, enraged glare
    of the born disciplinarian,
while all the while the neck's
spiral tube's atremble,
    for the bird, too, is fearful. . . .


    Through hesitancy we are placed
in kinship with the scarred rat
    as it hungrily sniffs at
the broken cellar window;
    elsewhere, with the chary
candy-striped spider as
    with an evenhanded
        sinister dexterity
    it sidesteps fatefully
toward that wobble in the web
that may mean prey, or
    may mean predator.

A joint appeal in all
things subject to a contrary
        pull—as in the very
faint, loose-lipped whistle
        of a warming kettle, or that
blackened buried moment when
        a cloudburst's certain
                but still nothing, not a drop,
        spills, or the hairline
fissure's inchmeal venture
down the flume's granite wall—
        links our comical, our pretzel-


                necked ostrich, so far
from its home, with the rupturing
        perilous push of a king-
side pawn: a mere one-square
        advance along the board's
periphery, and yet a move
        hazarded only upon
                long mulling within
        the miniaturized viscera
of a grandmaster computer.
For pause links with pause,
        or will at least for those

yearning to feel that these
things, too, go with some minimal
reluctance, don't just tumble
—so much deadweight cargo—
down and down in projectable
collisions, forever locked
in the straitened chute
of strict causality . . . but know
in every pressing second
second thoughts, and a doubt
turned wishful: *if we are not free,*
*we would like to be.*

Colder than snow

is how it feels, the year's first rain,
falling on a dark afternoon
the last week of January.

The neon signs

downtown already are blinking,
probably, patchily tinting
the hoods of cars, the ample crowns

of umbrellas

afloat on a washed-in clamor
of honks, whistles, shouts; but here,
upstairs in an old wooden house

five miles away

on the abrupt edge of Kyoto's eastern
line of hills, the darkness and the rain
alike come peacefully down.

It's an old house

that seems older as the rain falls,
rooting out from the walls
a resin whose power it is

to dim all signs—

the strings of dental floss, books
and sweatpants, empty donut box,
stubby pot-bellied hash pipe,


maps and wayworn

backpack—of the current
American tenant,
as if to restore this room to those


whose once it was. . . .

This salvaging illusion (that it's
only time which separates
past from present, and the links still there


by which we might,

stooping, enter yet-simpler houses in
this old capital city, old even then,
of a castled nation whose moat


was the salt sea

itself) is unshaken
by the click-clatter, as of wooden
shoes, of a tall schoolgirl, scooting

along, holding
an opened magazine over her hair,
or by sounds of a distant car,
groaning, as any horse would,

at the steepness
of the hill. The city's
fading, or falling, or folding inwards as,
moonlessly, the cold outspreads itself;

those streams running
freely in the streets will be locked
in ice tonight. It's difficult
not to view this weather

as anything
other than a deepening
tightening, a fiercer colder gripping
of the ground by winter. . . . Only if

you close your eyes
as though about to sleep,
or in truth to sleep,
will the new year's first rain

perhaps summon

that long-gone and looked-for season
for which so many subterranean
spring-wound clocks are set; probably

    only to those,

if any, at the shivering limit
of consciousness is it
evident how a colossal, exquisite

    mathematical

accounting even now's in preparation,
a one-to-one correlation
whereby each raindrop's knocking shall

    have its answer—

together when, then, under
some newly exploded sun, each tight blossom
opens like a door.

In old Minako Wada's house
Everything has its place,
And mostly out of sight:
     Bedding folded away
     All day, brought down
     From the shelf at night,


     Tea things underneath
Low tea table and tablecloth—
And sliding screen doors,
     Landscape-painted, that hide
     Her clothes inside a wash
     Of mountains. Here, the floors


     Are a clean-fitting mosaic,
Mats of a texture like
A broom's; and in a niche
     In the tearoom wall
     Is a shrine to all of her
     Ancestors, before which


     She sets each day
A doll-sized cup of tea,
A doll-sized bowl of rice.
     She keeps a glass jar
     Of crickets that are fed fish
     Shavings, an eggplant slice,

And whose hushed chorus,
Like the drowsy toss
Of a baby's rattle, moves in
    On so tranquil a song
  It's soon no longer heard.
  The walls are thin


  In Minako Wada's little house,
Open to every lifting voice
On the street—by day, the cries
    Of the children, at night
  Those excited, sweet,
  Reiterated goodbyes


  Of men full of beer who now
Must hurry home. Just to
Wake in the night inside this nest,
    Late, the street asleep (day done,
  Day not yet begun), is what
  Perhaps she loves best.

These light-footed, celebrated
 cats, created
on gold-leaf screens by a man
 who'd never seen a tiger
 (there were none in Japan),
who worked, as he'd been taught,
from pelts, and from paintings brought
 from distant, brilliant China,

 wander an extraordinary
 maze whose very
air's alive, alit with breeze-
 borne inebriants. It's a place
 of tumbled boundaries
and whetted penchants, in which
big-chested brutes whose eyes are rich
 outsize eggs of burnished gold,

 whose coats are cloudy, glowing
 masses flowing
behind an emerald palisade
 of bamboo and the row
 of darker palings made
by their own sable bands, glide
fatefully in the failing light, wide
 mouths agape and bared teeth flashing.

It's an hour of satisfying
runs and flying
ambitions, as gravity's
traction relaxes a little
and hunting tigers freeze
into a fine, deepening
tensity, muscles marshaling
toward that signal opportune instant


when the commanding soul emerges:
*Now*—
*Now,* it urges,
and the breaking body slides
upon the air's broad back
and hangs there, rides and rides
with limbs outstretched—but claws
bedded in their velvet-napped paws,
for there will be no killings tonight.


*All bloodshed is forbidden*
*here....*
That's the hidden
message of these grounds, which threads
like a stream around the pines
and rocks and iris-beds.
The danger's all a bluff, an
artful dumb show staged by a clan-
destine family of tigers

with Chinese dragon faces,
  whose grimaces
and slashing, cross-eyed glances serve
  to conceal the grins that beckon
    you into the preserve
of a rare, ferociously
playful mind. Enter. You are free
  from harm here. There's nothing to fear.

# IN A JAPANESE MOSS GARDEN

After a night of rain
    this garden so
fragile it's never raked, but swept,
    lies on a bed
soft as itself, and all the morning, fed
by the rain banked richly below,
    bathes in a glow


    gentle as candle-light.
        Variety's
ascendant in this lowland where
    a hundred-plus
plush samples of the like-velutinous—
star-shaped mosses, amulets, keys,
    bells, snowflakes—ease


    toward freshly minted greens
        which have no one-
word names: rust- or russet-green, pump-
        kin-tangerine-,
copper- and pewter-, frost- and fire-green. . . .
No land was ever overrun
    more mildly, none

yielded with more repose:
an intertwined,
inclusive, inch-by-inch advance
built this retreat
where stones are put to rest beneath a sheet
of nap, where limbs are under-lined,
and where the mind


meets not tranquility
merely, but some
dim image of itself—the rounded
mounds, the seams dense
with smaller seams, the knit, knobbed filaments
all suggesting the cranium,
as witnessed from


within. But now this web
of imagery
bends with a newcomer the colors
of an unripe
tomato who, beast of another stripe,
untended and rootlessly free,
apparently,

runs, runs, runs without rest.
His body gleams
with those pellucid lusters found
within a night's
last vistas, when a dyeing dawn alights
upon your lids, flooding your dreams,
until it seems


your inborn sights and pigments
outshine the day;
it's morning in a Japanese
moss garden and
a creature blazing like a firebrand
now makes its episodic way
between a gray


stand of toadstools that lean
like headstones, through
a swampy heel-print, up a fallen
leaf (and then back
down when it proves an airy cul-de-sac),
across a root, a stump, a dew-
drenched avenue

of shorter moss that looks
       and feels like felt. . . .
Inanimate, the garden may
       better have met
the thoughtful ends on which its lines are set,
but if its motionlessness must
       come to a halt,


       what cause more fitting than
              this zigzag creature,
bizarre as anything in Nature,
       whose home's a firma-
mental network, a plane of lifelines pitched
upon a random set of reference
       points, a maze which in its


       closed-in stringiness makes
              a self-portrait?
One might view him as captive, too,
       like any prey
inside his web, yet still take heart at the way
he runs to the task, as if to say,
       Today's the very


       day for weaving finally
              a tapestry
at once harmonious and true.

# A FLIGHT FROM OSAKA

Into the translucent, smudged, omnivorous wheel
    That the propeller's become
Now slides, block on block and brightly unreal,
    The highflung reaches of sun-dazed Kobe,
        On whose big bay

On this early-summer Sunday afternoon some
    Playfully downscaled freighters
Are lugging broad, ballooning wakes in from
    And out to sea. . . . Quite a leisurely scene
        (Or so when seen

From a few miles up), with one neat, upending touch
    Of real loveliness: the way
Those wakes suggest jet streams—only so much
    Slower to gather, to shatter, to wear
        Themselves out where

Each least impulse is translated into a dense,
    Earthbound medium. The weight,
The piled resistance of those depths, presents
    Us with another, plainer image: one
        Of a hard-won

And never finished struggle with a stone- and vine-
    Strewn soil, a primitive plow
Scratching out, foot by foot, its thin lifeline—
    Into which our buried forebears scattered seeds.
        The past recedes

Much as the circling world does from the round
    Windows of a plane, expanding
As it dwindles into the background, turning
    Both more mysterious and more finely
        Drawn, finally.

# SEASIDE GREETINGS

(OKI ISLANDS, JAPAN SEA)

Together waking to the smell
of new mats beneath us, we find our clothes,
quickly dress, and in slippers shuffle
    down the dark hall

    to the entryway, where we trade
slippers for shoes, slide the front
door free, and steal outside
    without a sound.

    Our fishing village has not woken
much before us; day is in the splendid,
splashy process of breaking
    over an open

    sea and over flooded ricefields
become lavender mirrors, snugly
secured by little green studs.
    We have big pads

    of paper bundled under our arms — off
to sketch Yoroi Iwa,
Armor Rock, the crest of a bluff
    which, just as if

    something with endless time to kill
on this outpost island had been
engineering an epochal
    if rather small

joke, not only looks like armor but in
its boxy, braided lines is closer
to the Japanese style than
　　　the European.

Of course given the scale Nature has
to work with, all of these uncanny,
and often funny, resemblances
　　　(the ancient trees

　　wrung like buxom women, whales
in the clouds, bights like laughing
horses' heads, potatoes bearing profiles
　　　of generals

　　dead now for centuries) are
statistical certainties, nothing
more, and yet they do appease our
　　　appetite for

　　play at the stone heart of things—
a loose, elusive spirit not
about to shimmer its mica wings
　　　in our smudged drawings.

Under a midday sun we climb
a treeless, grasshopper-ridden hill
whose summit drops headlong as doom
　　　to the torn rim

of the sea a hundred yards or so
below. Hawks ride in the updrafts
and test us with unnervingly
     low, virtuoso

     swoops and passes, so near we can discern
how the jumpy eyes pivot in their heads.
Their motions have no waste—glide and turn
     as though they're borne

     upon a refined physics,
an applied mathematics streamlining
toward the pure. We watch their slow arcs
     and plunging strikes,

     cheered to see them flutter
up with empty claws; while nothing we've
ever seen goes about the search for
     a meal with more

     inspiriting grace, our sympathies
are with the homely, camouflage-
seeking mouse, rather than with these
     ferocious beauties.

     . . . Dusk is something taking place
at unreachable distances,
moving off at one remove from us,
     who raptly focus,

with the fixity of the deservedly
ravenous, on the feast being set
before us—rice, squash, spinach in soy
    and sesame,

    sweet ribbons of squid strewn
with pinhead-sized pink fish eggs, pickles,
a sea-bream sliced for sashimi and then
    fitted back in

    around the bones to restore
its swimming shape, a clear soup, bamboo
shoots, lotus root, and two half-liter
    bottles of beer.

    Loaned kimono-like robes hold in
the heat from our baths as we eat,
and as we retire to an embracing
    sudden exhaustion

    larger than we are. Within
each other's arms we lie, neatly, indeed
almost palindromically, placed: settling
    *in in an inn.* . . .

The phrase, nearly perfect, is perfect for
tomorrow's postcards, those shiny seaviews
for our friends that might begin, "Dear _____,
    It's lovely here."

# ON A SEASIDE MOUNTAIN

(OKI ISLANDS, JAPAN SEA)

Earlier, as if to conform
to our distant notions of what a remote
Japanese island ought to look like, a warm
sea-mist sifted in, transmuting browns and greens

into the hovering, washed-out grays
of one of those old vertical landscapes
whose ascent to the temple threads a double maze
of fog and foliage. Yet as we climb

from the coast, slips of color filter through—
a red swatch of earth, freshly torn, a green red-
berried bush, green-gold clumps of bamboo—
and the waves' gentle papery crash drifts out

of hearing. To know that the Japanese
seven and again six hundred years ago
banished powerful emperors to these
very islands enriches the mist; far as such

kingdoms are, they'll never be nearer
than while the ground's unreally webbed with fog,
like this, and the air's a breathed-on mirror.
The hills hold, visibly, a second tale,

one—small-plotted, cyclical—of buried toil:
the scaling eye still traces terraces
where rice was grown by hand, and by the handful.
    Ahead, a fall of sunlight, washing some

of the mist from the air, unveils a crust
of prisms on a big rock outcrop. The cloud
cover's coming brightly undone at last.
It's rainbow weather. The bands are there, just

waiting for the right touch of sun.
Yet as we round another bend, the sight we're
treated to is something else again:
a horse, a chunky tan palomino

with milky mane and a calm, discerning
fix to the eyes. The creature stamps, as if
commanding us to halt, which we do, returning
its gauging stare. It expels a long, low

importunate snuffle; then, as if it wants
to make itself perfectly clear, repeats
this sound and, ears up, waits on our response.
None forthcoming, it rears its head, utters a keen

unnerving squeal that seems to hold a bit
of laughter, plunges around (admitting
a glimpse of bobbing genitals, as this *it*
becomes a *he*) and clatters off. . . . He doesn't

go far. A short ways up the mountainside
he stops for us—until we near. Again he's
gone; again he stops. He's become our guide,
apparently. In any case, we follow him

while the remaining mist burns into the sun
until we reach a circular outlook high
above the sea, where nine horses, including one
pony whose mane's so short it stands erect, are

grazing. Head down, duties done, our leader glides
in among his comely fellows, none of whom
show much alarm at having us at their sides.
They huddle closer perhaps, but, snouts in clover,

carry on with the business of the day.
It's so quiet we can hear their surf-like breathing.
   Below, though worn white at the rim of the bay,
the sea by sheer drops precipitately builds

toward an unsounded blue, deeper than the sky's,
richer than mist or history. Whenever
one of these horses lifts its thoughtful eyes
from the turf, stems trailing from its mouth,

this is the view. They eat slowly. The sun's pace
is perfectly theirs, and the planted ease
they are breathing, are breeding, in this place,
while not meant for us, lightens us anyway.

# A NOTE ABOUT THE AUTHOR

Brad Leithauser was born in Michigan in 1953 and grew up there. After graduating from Harvard College and Harvard Law School, he spent several years in Japan, where he was a research fellow at the Kyoto Comparative Law Center. He was Visiting Writer at Amherst College for the academic year 1984–85, and now lives in Italy with his wife, the poet Mary Jo Salter, and their daughter, Emily.

His previous collection of poetry, *Hundreds of Fireflies,* was published in 1982, and his novel, *Equal Distance,* in 1985. His poems and critical articles have appeared in *The New Yorker, The Atlantic Monthly, Harper's, The New Republic,* and *The New Criterion,* among other periodicals. He is the recipient of many awards for his writing, including a Guggenheim Fellowship, an Ingram-Merrill grant, an Amy Lowell Poetry Travelling Scholarship, and a MacArthur Fellowship.

A NOTE ON THE TYPE

The text of this book was set in film in a typeface called Griffo, a camera version of Bembo, the well-known monotype face. The original cutting of Bembo was made by Francesco Griffo of Bologna only a few years after Columbus discovered America. It was named for Pietro Bembo, the celebrated Renaissance writer and humanist scholar who was made a cardinal and served as secretary to Pope Leo X. Sturdy, well balanced, and finely proportioned, Bembo is a face of rare beauty. It is, at the same time, extremely legible in all of its sizes.

Composed by Superior Type,
Champaign, Illinois

Printed and bound by Halliday Lithographers,
West Hanover, Massachusetts

Typography and binding by Marysarah Quinn,
based on a design by Joe Marc Freedman